Landforms

Mountains

Cassie Mayer

Heinemann
LIBRARY

H www.heinemann.co.uk/library

Visit our website to find out more information about Heinemann Library books.

To order:

☎ Phone 44 (0) 1865 888066
  Send a fax to 44 (0) 1865 314091
📄 Visit the Heinemann Bookshop at www.heinemann.co.uk/library to browse our
💻 catalogue and order online.

First published in Great Britain by Heinemann Library,
Halley Court, Jordan Hill, Oxford OX2 8EJ, part of Harcourt
Education. Heinemann is a registered trademark of Harcourt
Education Ltd.

Editorial: Tracey Crawford, Cassie Mayer, Dan Nunn,
  and Sarah Chappelow
Design: Jo Hinton-Malivoire
Picture Research: Heather Mauldin and Tracy Cummins
Production: Duncan Gilbert

Originated by Chroma Graphics (Overseas) Pte. Ltd
Printed and bound in China by South China
Printing Company

ISBN 978 0 431 18231 5 (hardback)
11 10 09 08 07
10 9 8 7 6 5 4 3 2 1

ISBN 978 0 431 18354 1 (paperback)
12 11 10 09 08
10 9 8 7 6 5 4 3 2 1

British Library Cataloguing in Publication Data
Mayer, Cassie
  Mountains. - (Landforms)
  1.Mountains - Juvenile literature
  I.Title
  551.4'32

Acknowledgements
The publishers would like to thank the following for permission
to reproduce photographs: Alamy p. 13 (John.Cleare/Mountain.
Camera); Corbis pp. 4 (river, Pat O'Hara; volcano, Galen Rowell;
island, George Steinmetz; cave, Layne Kennedy), 5 (Royalty Free),
6 (George Steinmetz), 7 (Joseph Sohm/Visions of America), 8
(Yann Arthus-Bertrand), 11 (Galen Rowell), 12 (Sheldan Collins), 16
(Skyscan), 17 (Kazuyoshi Nomachi), 18 (George H. H. Huey), 19
(SIME), 20 (Galen Rowell), 23 (Galen Rowell); Getty Images pp. 9
(ED Darack), 10 (David Wall), 14 (Richard Olsenius), 15 (David
Paterson), 23 (both, Wall); Jupiter p. 21 (Solstice Photography).

Cover photograph of clouds over the Rocky Mountains, Canada,
reproduced with permission of FLPA/Foto Natura (Will Meinderts).
Backcover image of a sandstone formation reproduced with
permission of Getty Images/Richard Olsenius.

Every effort has been made to contact copyright holders of any
material reproduced in this book. Any omissions will be rectified in
subsequent printings if notice is given to the publishers.

Contents

Landforms

The land is made of different shapes.
These shapes are called landforms.

mountain

A mountain is a landform.
Mountains are found all over the world.

What is a mountain?

A mountain is land that rises up from the ground.

rock

Mountains are very high and rocky.

Some mountains are in warm countries.

Some mountains are in cold countries.

Features of a mountain

peak

base

The top of a mountain is called the peak. The bottom of a mountain is called the base.

When lots of mountains are close together, it is called a range.

How mountains change

Mountains change over time. Over millions of years, wind, ice, and water shape the mountain.

Wind blows the soil off the mountain.
Water and ice wear away the rock.

Types of mountain

Some mountains have steep slopes and pointed peaks.

Some mountains have gentle slopes and rounded peaks.

Some mountains are underwater.
The peak of this mountain sticks out
of the water.

Some mountains have strangely
shaped rocks.

What lives on a mountain?

mountain lion

Plants and animals live on mountains.
This mountain lion lives on a mountain
in Colorado, USA.

Some people live on mountains too.
This village is built on the side of a
mountain in Switzerland.

Visiting mountains

People like to visit mountains.
Some people like to walk up the
mountain paths.

Some people like to climb
mountains and look down
on the land below.

Mountain facts

Ben Nevis is the highest
mountain in the United Kingdom.
It is 1344 metres high.

Mount Everest is the highest
mountain in the world.
It is in Asia. It is 8850 metres high.

Picture glossary

base the bottom of a mountain

peak the top of a mountain

range a group of mountains

Index

Notes to parents and teachers

Before reading

Talk about mountains. Explain that they are landforms which rise high above the ground. Some mountains have snow on their peaks, even in hot countries!

After reading

Make a mountain range. Help the children to draw a range of mountain peaks on a roll of lining paper. Cover the higher mountain peaks with white textured wallpaper to represent snow caps. Colour in the higher slopes in brown and the lower slopes in green. Help the children to label some of the mountain bases and peaks.

Sing the song: The Bear Went Over the Mountain.

The bear went over the mountain (repeat 3 times)

To see what he could see.

But all that he could see (2 times)

Was...the other side of the mountain (2 times)

Was all that he could see!

Encourage the children to look at websites featuring Mount Everest. Can they find out what it looks like at the top?